THE WORLD'S MOST TERRIFYING PREDATORS

PART 2

By Justin & Peter Hoke

The World's Most Terrifying Predators Part 2

By Justin Hoke

To Sam, Peter, and Joshua

Printed in the United States of America

First Printing, 2023

The King Cobra

The king cobra lives in Asia.

They eat small animals such as
mice and lizards.

They are very good at biting their prey and using venom to kill them.

They can live up to 20 years.

The Hyena

The hyena lives in Africa.

They eat meat, such as wildebeests and zebras.

They are very good at hunting in packs and can run very fast.

They can live up to 25 years.

The Cheetah

The cheetah lives in Africa.

They eat meat, such as gazelles and antelopes.

They are the fastest land animal in the world and can run up to 70 miles per hour.

They can live up to 12 years.

The Hippopotamus

The hippopotamus lives in Africa.

They eat grass and plants.

They are very strong and can run
very fast.

They can live up to 50 years.

The Red-tailed Hawk

The red-tailed hawk lives in North America.

They eat small animals such as mice and rabbits.

They are very good at flying and swooping down to catch their prey.

They can live up to 25 years.

The Tasmanian Devil

The Tasmanian devil lives in Australia.

They eat meat, such as birds and small animals.

They are very good at biting their prey and can be very aggressive.

They can live up to 5 years.

The Scorpion

The scorpion lives in many different parts of the world.

They eat small animals such as insects.

They are very good at using their stinger to kill their prey.

They can live up to 8 years.

THE END